FINISH STRONG

Authored by Pastor Carl Flowers

Trinity Outreach Publishing
502 Jarrell St
Picayune, MS 39466

Copyright © 2016 by Carl Flowers

Take note that the name satan and related names are not capitalized. We choose not to acknowledge him, even to the point of violating grammatical rules.

For information address Trinity Outreach Publishing Rights Department, 502 Jarrell St, Picayune, MS 39466

First Paperback edition September 2016

Manufactured in the United States of America

ISBN-13: 978-0692779583

ISBN-10: 0692779582

It is my prayer that this will be made available to Christian bookstores and distributors worldwide.

DEDICATION

To the most caring and wonderful woman in the world, my precious wife, Julie, for her increasing Love and commitment to me, our Family, and the Kingdom of God.

To my son, Justin, to my Daughter Tayla, to my grandchildren, Ra'Nyra, Jaidyn, and Nova Flowers.

To my church family and staff at Trinity Outreach Ministries, who faithfully loved and supported me over the years.

To my Mother Joyce I Mclaurin, who has faithfully labored, physically and prayerfully on my behalf.

In memory of my uncles, Cornelius (Sonny) McLaurin and Chirley McLaurin, and to the great mentors and protégé's of inspiration who will never be forgotten for the impact they have made on my life.

I dedicate this book to the great men of my family: Victor, Jesse, Charles, Christopher Zac McLaurin, DJ McLaurin, Fredrick Turner, and my son, Justin Flowers who are all great athletes and fathers.

To the Men of Destiny at Trinity Outreach Ministries.

To my spiritual father, Apostle Jimmy Peters, and to all the leaders and Coaches who invested in my life.

To all the men and women who look to me as a father and mentor; because of you, this book has come to fruition.

To my Lord and Savior, who has delivered and set me free, who has made all things possible for me.

I dedicate this book to whoever has struggled in life with addiction, who wants to learn how to win in the Finals of life. I encourage you to Finish Strong. Totally surrender to Jesus Christ as your Lord and Savior.

~Apostle Carl Flowers~

FORWARD

I have witnessed, a prime example of someone who has continuously gained momentum throughout this race called life.

My Father has been my biggest inspirations for the slogan, "Finish Strong", over the past 20 years and I filmy believe experience is the best teacher. It did not surprise me when my Dad announced that the title of his 2nd book was going to be, "Finish Strong", hearing this phase repeatedly by him throughout my childhood. I've witnessed many ups and downs in my father's life, along with a life that has been full of, peaks and valleys itself.

I truly believe this book, "FINISH STRONG", will motivate, uplift, and inspire anyone who may need some extra inspiration in this race called life. Not only for the uninspired or lost, but it is also a very positive message that should be shared and read.

I, as the son of Pastor Carl Flowers, can vouch that he has been true in his intent and has nothing but great intentions as he, humble, but aggressively, stays focused on helping people for the good, and spreading the word of God.

-Son of Author, J. Flowers

I would get off of the bus about 60 yards from my house on Rosetta Ct and line up next to the bus digging my feet into the dirt road. I would look up at Freda and wait until she was finished letting everyone off of the bus and close the double doors. She would glance over at me and smile and then "rev up" the bus engine a little and take off down the street. I would race her to the edge of my yard and sometimes she would let me win and other times she would beat me by a few feet being sure to blow the horn on the bus twice as she laughed and continued to drive to the next stop on the corner.

I was in 5th grade at Auburn Heights Elementary school and my love for running and racing was being ignited by a school bus driver that probably never knew the impact she had on me. Coach Collins was a very reserved, serious, and no nonsense kind of a guy who happened to take a special interest in a small group of misguided and somewhat immature high school underclassmen. Maybe he saw some potential in us or maybe he was just bored and had some extra time on his hands. Regardless, he introduced us to the indoor track circuit and gave us the opportunity to prepare for the upcoming track season by competing against college athletes from all over the state of Michigan. I probably would have quit at some point but Carl's energy and enthusiasm somehow kept me going into the beginning of our freshman year on Avondale's varsity track team. We would eventually compete in and win many races individually and together on relay teams over the course of our high school career.

Carl Flowers, Dave Kapanowki, and I were all running down Old Squirrel Road toward Oakland University enjoying the cool spring weather and lack of traffic present during those days. We were laughing, being silly, and running like we had been doing for the past couple of years as teammates. Carl was always leading the pack and pushing us to run faster and longer than we really wanted to but we did it anyway because we knew we had to finish together. It wouldn't be long before Dave and Carl had graduated from high school and I was left to fend for myself as a senior on the track team. I didn't have my friends there to push me in person but I could always hear Carl in the back of my mind telling me to go faster and work harder, which I did most of the time. I ended up having a great season and finished strong just like Carl and Dave would have expected. I applied that same "never give up" philosophy/attitude to my time spent in the United States Army and I have tried to inspire my students that I have taught for the past 20 years to think and behave in a similar manner.

I miss my friends and I hope one day we will be able to get back together for maybe one last run. I guess I better start getting in shape just in case that happens in the near future. Carl is already leading the pack again by sharing his latest accomplishments in regards to losing weight and getting himself in shape. I know that he would say that all things are possible through God and that I need to get up off of the couch and finish strong. I may just do that.

By: Tracy Johnson

To my teammate, RB partner and good friend. First let me say that I love you and thank you for being you. From our preteen years to today I am privileged and honored to be able to call you a true friend. We both came from single parent homes, we had strong hard working Christian mothers who prayed for us daily and only wanted what was best for their sons. In terms of sports and finding ourselves as teenagers, Carl and I really leaned on each other, talked hours on the phone and challenged each other to be the best that we could be. I knew Carl was up running and lifting weights so it was imperative that I woke up and did the same. With that being said, congratulations on your book and I salute you my brother. God Bless.

By: Ritchie Garrett
Football Coach
Avondale High School

PREFACE

Can a Christian Become
Disqualified?

Is ONCE saved...ALWAYS saved?

How does a Christian stay in shape
for the Kingdom of Heaven?

How do we finish STRONG?

FINISH STRONG

Table of Contents

Hebrews 12:1-2 - Wherefore seeing we also are compassed about with so great a cloud of witnesses, let us lay aside every weight, and the sin which doth so easily beset us, and let us run with patience the race that is set before us, ² Looking unto Jesus the author and finisher of our faith; who for the joy that was set before him endured the cross, despising the shame, and is set down at the right hand of the throne of God.

I.THE DISCIPLINE

In order to be a great athlete one must be disciplined, teachable, and motivated. It is the same with running the Christian race. We must resort to our strength in the Lord to achieve the victory.

II. THE DIRECTION

Each athlete as a new believer in Christ has to have a heart for God's direction.

III. THE DETERMINATION

Life brings about a challenge to every believer. There are highs and lows in each life span but we must continue in the faith and pursue the finish line.

Go for the Gold!!

Finish Strong!!

With a diligent spirit, the Bible says we walk by faith and not by sight. With that being said, we cannot allow things to detour us out of our lane. Men of God, women of God, I encourage you to stay in your lane as you continue to grow in Christ Jesus. You will endure to the end. The goal, the mark is heaven. The bible said all have sinned and come short of the Glory of God. We have missed the mark in our sin. We have missed the mark in our shame. But through Jesus Christ we can achieve the glory. The glory is that we have eternity with Christ Jesus. For the Bible says that God so loved the world that He gave his only begotten son that whoever believes in Him shall not perish but shall have everlasting life. That is a promise to the believer. That is a promise when you enter this race. It is the promise of victory.

Today, you can have the victory. No matter what happened in your life, no matter what disqualified you from being a productive citizen, now you too can learn about the grace of God. You can also condition yourself to stay in the will of God.

There is a lot of erroneous teaching that's going forth in the world. Or should I say erroneous doctrine that has been taught by religion. I will like to say this, if our religion don't change us, we need to change our religion. So this book is to encourage you to stay in the race, but most importantly, to finish strong.

Finish strong as being a father. Finish strong as being a mother. Finish strong as being a productive Christian. Serve your church well. Serve your leadership team well. Be productive. Live life more abundantly. Be happy. Endure the pain. Endure hardness as a good soldier. Be all you can be in this Christian race.

God bless and finish strong.

I mentioned unto you in my last book that I was disqualified to serve in the United States Army because of a bad eyesight, even though I was physically ready. I served my unit before basic training, I passed the ASVAB test. I sang the military songs, I ran the military long country miles, and I prepared myself for the goal of becoming a drill instructor. My MOS was Bravo 10 Infantry right out on the front line but my dreams were soon shattered. With the disqualification due to my eyesight came disappointment as well as a log flight back home.

I wrote to my congressman but there was nothing they could do. I was disqualified, right then and right there. Even though I wasn't able to achieve my military dreams, I am fulfilling my Kingdom dreams. I am in shape for the Kingdom of God, I am a drill instructor, and I am a good soldier in the Lord running this Christian race.

- **The Christian life is a difficult marathon that we must run.**
- **To run the Christian marathon, we must get into shape and stay in shape.**
- **To run the Christian marathon, we must run with endurance the course set before us.**
- **The encouragement to keep running comes from those who have run before us, but primarily from Jesus Himself.**
- **We run with endurance by fixing our eyes on Jesus.**

Hebrews 12:1-2 - Wherefore seeing we also are compassed about with so great a cloud of witnesses, let us lay aside every weight, and the sin which doth so easily beset us, and let us run with patience the race that is set before us, ² Looking unto Jesus the author and finisher of our faith; who for the joy that was set before him endured the cross, despising the shame, and is set down at the right hand of the throne of God.

Lay Aside All Weights

This refers to a runner making sure that all extra weights have been removed from his body. I once was a 279 pound man. I wasn't ready to run a marathon. I had to trim down and condition myself physically.

In doing so I had to change my eating habits, I had to have mental preparation in order to strive in the physical activity. I had to lay aside the extra weight. I had to trim the fat.

In the spiritual arena, this refers to anything that hinders our walk with God. It speaks of things that are innocent in and of themselves, but when they slow you down in the Christian race, they are weights and they must go. The list of these things could be endless, but a few are: Our addictions, cocaine, methamphetamine, pornography , cigarettes, works of the flesh , sin to the body, things entering our eye gates, the lust of the flesh, and the lust of the eye in the pride of life. These things will disqualify anyone. ALL have sinned and come short of the glory.

Lay Aside All Sins

Next, the author encourages his readers to get rid of "besetting sins". This refers to sins which cling to, distracts, entangles and trips the Christian runner. The picture is of a man trying to run a race while dressed in the long flowing robes of the day. It would be easy for him to be tripped up and fall out of the race. The Bible tells us not to be entangled with the yoke of bondage.

There are many sins that could be mentioned at this point, but the idea in this verse is that particular sin which trips you up. You know where you are weak. There are sins that do not tempt you at all, but there are others that are a constant source of temptation. This is what the writer is referring to here. Whatever that sin is, it must be stripped off and avoided at all costs. Else, it will entangle you, trip you and prevent you from finishing your race!

Romans 6:12 - *Let not sin therefore reign in your mortal body, that ye should obey it in the lusts thereof.*

We Must Run With Patience

Here the picture is of a runner settling in for the long haul. However, it is not a picture of sitting back and waiting to see what will come our way in life. It is an active word that tells speaks of a person who has a spirit in him that stands up and faces the trials of life.

He goes forth and runs at trouble. He conquers it and over comes it in the power of the Lord. He is able to face his trials because he knows the Lord has brought it to him for his own good and for God's glory.

Romans 8:28 - *And we know that all things work together for good to them that love God, to them who are the called according to his purpose.*

As I write about physical condition versus spiritual condition, which there is some similarities, it's a requirement that we give an effort and dedicate ourselves either way.

I will talk about our physical conditioning first. Physically we have to prepare ourselves and it's something that you can do. It is something you can get control of. It is something you can prepare for and scope your body, build up your endurance, your wind capacity, and your flexibility. But you have to be determined, and it's going to take an effort.

Spiritually, faith without works is dead. If you don't do anything, you won't get any results. With that being said, it's going to take determination and it's going to take consistency. For instance, if you were to begin to set a goal to walk every day, there will be results simply because you made an effort. If you want to achieve your goals, you have to continue to persevere in the process.

Walking in my neighborhood, I was determined to get myself in shape physically as well as spiritually. I used that time as meditation and concentration. I turn my walking into prayer walks. It's a time that I can meditate on the goodness of God and prioritize my day, focus on my evenings, and pretty much examine myself, whether or not I'm in shape or what I need to do to improve.

By the time I left Cozumel, Mexico, I was way out of shape physically. I was wearing 279 pounds. What I decided to do when I got back was to begin an exercise routine that would help improve my physical conditions.

So, I began the arduous process of walking. I started out with two miles per day, walking in my neighborhood. I would download an app called "Map My Walk" which had a GPS, and I would walk pretty much every day in different directions to break the monotony, and set my pace to achieve higher goals.

I did great for the first week. It took mental preparation. It took determination. It took me making effort. With that being said, every week I would increase my knowledge. I would set higher goals. I would build up my heart rate. I began to walk, and then my walking turning into jogging. That is a process. It takes determination. That broke the cycle of complacency. That broke the cycle of mediocracy.

I think every believer, every athlete, has to be determined. You have to make up your own mind, and you have to be motivated. Motivation comes through your mental ability to encourage yourself.

"Finish Strong" is a book that will discipline your spirit man to stay in condition. It is compared to an athlete versus our Christian race. There are powerful scriptures that will take you to your goal and help you press towards the mark of the prize of the high calling, which is in Christ Jesus.

We must understand that we have to work out our own soul salvation with fear and trembling, and we can fall from grace out of the will of God into a backslidden state.

We will discover some insightful scriptures that we have to stay fit for the kingdom of God, and stay in relationship with God in His word that we can be productive Christians in our everyday life.

I pray that this book will be very insightful to you, as it has been a blessing for me to finish this book. To encourage you how I disciplined myself to maintain the strength to endure to the end. Stay encouraged. You might be dealing with the preliminaries of life, or the semi-finals in life and ready for the finals of life. I pray that this book prevents you from being disqualified, or should I say, fallen out of the will of God, or fallen from grace, or even in a backslidden state.

You will read the Truth, and it's the Truth that will set you free. I pray that this book be a blessing to you. With a diligent spirit, the Bible says we walk by faith and not by sight. With that being said, we cannot allow things to detour us out of our lane. Men of God, women of God, I encourage you to stay in your lane as you continue to grow in Christ Jesus. You will endure to the end. The goal, the mark, is heaven. The Bible says all have sinned and come short of the Glory of God.

We have missed the mark in our sin. We have missed the mark in our shame. But through Jesus Christ we can achieve the glory. The glory is we have eternity with Christ Jesus. For the Bible says that God so loved the world that he gave his only begotten Son that whoever believes in him shall not perish but shall have everlasting life. That is a promise to the believer. That is a promise when you enter this race. It is a promise of VICTORY!

Today, you can have the victory! No matter what happened in your life, no matter what disqualified you from being a productive citizen, now you, too, can learn about the grace of God. You can also condition yourself to stay in the will of God.

I can remember as a young athlete starting off running track how I made some very unfortunate mistakes at the beginning. In some races, I jumped the gun and started off too fast. Than in other races, I was too slow. As a result, my actions caused me to be disqualified.

I had the opportunity of having great coaches who mentored me who showed me the proper form and proper technique in order to be competitive. In comparison to a Christian race, God will place people in your life to mentor you to help strengthen your Christian conduct to be all you can be.

But you have to have a teachable spirit, you have to be coachable or trainable, and also respectable in order to receive instructions to run into a Christian race. This race, it is not given to the strong or the swift, but to those that endure to the end.

We can become disqualified by stepping out of the will of God. I don't believe that once saved, always saved. The Bible speaks that we should work out our own soul salvation with fear and trembling. We can fall from grace. We can go back to our old sin like the prodigal son. We can waste our finances. We can waste our talents. We can waste our life in sin.

The Bible says all have sinned and have come short glory of the God and we want to be able to be strengthened that we may endure the trials that we go through in everyday life. We can't run from our troubles. Sometimes we have to run in amidst of our troubles.

With that being said, we have to have the word of God in our heart. The Bible tells us to be strong in the Lord in the power of his might. To put on the whole armor of God that we may be able to stand against the wiles of the Devil.

There will be test in our life on a daily basis. We will be tempted. We will go through the trials of life. Some people don't make it through the preliminaries. Some are not fortunate to make it to the semi-finals, and some even die before the finals. But the paradigm is, we can get strengthened today to live our life in an eternity with Jesus Christ.

This book "Finish Strong" will help you to strive for excellence. It will educate you spiritually with the fact that we have to stay in the will of God in order to qualify in the kingdom of God. We will be encouraged and enriched by the function of the Holy Spirit to continue to run in this race even when times get hard.

You are going to have some bad moments in the day, but it shouldn't ruin your whole day. The Bible tells us that man must always pray, and pray without ceasing. We are going to have to build up ourselves. We are going to have to condition ourselves for the long haul. We can't get fatigued and we cannot get burned out, but we are going to have to run this race.

We each have our own race to run!

That is, you cannot run in my lane and I cannot run in yours! I am convinced that the cause of Christ has been hindered by many who refuse to run in their own lane and they end up hindering everyone around them.

We are not in competition, but we are on the same team!

My job isn't to outrun you, my job is to run for Jesus, the race that He has planned for me to the best of my ability.

Our course has been individually designed!

The race you are running has been prepared just for you. The best thing we can do is run our race to the best of our God-given ability.

We Must Guard Our Priorities

Notice that verse 2a tells us that we are to run **"LOOKING UNTO JESUS THE AUTHOR AND FINISHER OF OUR FAITH."**

Plainly put, that means we are to use Jesus as our focal point while we run the race we have been given by God. You see, He ran His race, and He ran it well. He finished the course that was laid out for Him and now He stands as the supreme champion in the race of life. In fact, He is the race judge.

The race judge was the man who called the race. He decided who was disqualified and who was running well. While we run, we must not look at the other runners. Doing so will cause distraction and defeat. We must not look at circumstances. Doing so will result in distraction and defeat.

Our eyes are to be on the One who started us on this race, and the One who will greet us at the end of it. Our primary duty while we run is to look to Him. Anything less will spell disaster for the Christian runner. Focus, stay in your lane.

Hebrews 12:13 - Looking unto Jesus, the author and finisher of our faith; who for the joy that was set before him endured the cross, despising the shame, and is set down at the right hand of the throne of God. For consider him that endured such contradiction of sinners against himself, lest ye be wearied and faint in your minds.

Warming Up

We Must Make Proper Preparations

When there is a race to be run, the wise runner must make careful preparations. The same is true in a spiritual race as well. We will never reach our fullest potential for the Lord until we are willing to make the preparations and sacrifices that are necessary for running the race.

What area of your life do you find that you need the most encouragement?

_____

_____

_____

_____

_____

_____

_____

_____

_____

What would you find the most difficult about running a marathon? Would you rather run a marathon or a series of sprints? Why?

_____

_____

_____

_____

_____

_____

_____

_____

_____

Who do you think the writer is referring to
when he mentioned the great cloud of witnesses?

_____

_____

_____

_____

_____

_____

_____

_____

Why do you think the writer emphasized "the
great cloud of witnesses"? What might you learn
from the witnesses?

_____

_____

_____

_____

_____

_____

_____

_____

_____

What do you think the purpose of the great cloud of witnesses in our lives?

_____

_____

_____

_____

_____

_____

_____

_____

What do you think it means to live aside the way of sin that entangle us? What image or memories does the passage create in your mind?

_____

_____

_____

_____

_____

_____

_____

_____

_____

The scripture compares the Christian life to the running a race. How does the writer say we are supposed to run the race?

_____

_____

_____

_____

_____

_____

_____

_____

_____

Where are we to keep our eyes focused? Why is this so important?

_____

_____

_____

_____

_____

_____

_____

_____

_____

Write down the words used to describe the roles Jesus play when it comes to our faith. Identify and explain these two words.

_____
_____
_____
_____
_____
_____
_____
_____
_____

What was the finish line that motivated Jesus and allowed him to endure the race that was set before him?

_____
_____
_____
_____
_____
_____
_____
_____
_____

What did He just go through for us as he ran the race that the Father put before him?

_____
_____
_____
_____
_____
_____
_____
_____
_____

Who has encouraged you? Write down the names of your great cloud of witnesses.

_____
_____
_____
_____
_____
_____
_____
_____
_____

What is keeping you from running the race for Jesus? Confess those sins and strive to run in God's freedom.

_____
_____
_____
_____
_____
_____
_____
_____
_____

What is your Finish Line? What do you need to do to change your Finish Line and begin running in your lane for Jesus Christ?

_____
_____
_____
_____
_____
_____
_____
_____
_____

In the grandstands in heaven they are doing the Wave. They are shouting "Stay saved!" It is as if the saints who have gone before us, the heroes of faith that given their lives for the sake of Jesus Christ, they are surrounding us and cheering us on! Their lives stand as a testimony of faith and encourage us to run the race with excellence and endurance. They are many witnesses who died for their commitment to God who are now cheering us on. We need to examine our life now that we are entered into this race.

Where are you at now in life? Are you in the Preliminaries, the Semi Finals, or are you ready for the Finals?

_____

_____

_____

_____

_____

_____

_____

_____

I had the opportunity to compete in some major track and field events and state competitions during my high school years. A runner must be very disciplined. You must first stretch and flex and prepare your muscles for competition. During the track meet we had to qualify. We had the Preliminaries, the Semi-Finals and the Finals.

In all heats, winners will advance to the Semi-Finals. In addition, the next best times will advance to the Finals. For the races run in lanes, the number allowed to advance to the finals is limited by the number of lanes on the sectional track. The slowest times get the worst lanes and the best times get the best lanes. This also compares to a Christian race.

I had some agonies and defeats because I was disqualified by my sinful actions. This book, "Finish Strong", highlights how we need to stay in our lane and be all that we can be for the Kingdom of God.

If my devastating life struggles had not disqualified me, I would not have received Jesus Christ as my Lord and Savior. In track meets, I was disqualified many times. In life, I was out of condition, I wasn't fit to live and I wasn't fit to die; but still, the Lord saw fit to allow me qualification after my soul was conditioned through repentance.

We are called to a Christian race. It is not a sprint race, but we must condition ourselves to run spiritually. There is some false doctrine in the Christian race that states, "Once saved, always saved". This is just a figure of speech. I have found out in my personal life that I had to qualify to be a Christian by accepting Jesus Christ as my Lord and Savior. In doing so I had to live the life. It was more than just being called a Christian. I had to live a holy life. I had to obey God's word. I had to love what He loves and hate what he hate.

Being a newborn Christian, we have to have a personal relationship with Jesus Christ. We must be filled with the Holy Spirit in order to fulfil our destiny in the Kingdom of God. There are so many things that disqualified me that I had to receive instruction on how to run this race. The race is not given to the strong or the swift but to those endure to the end.

Is there any truth to the notion that once I give my life to God, I face no more jeopardy of Hell? Is it possible that once I obey the Gospel for the first time, I am never again at risk of being condemned?

Running the Race of Life!

You and I must live our lives governed by the word of God and the Holy Spirit. We didn't ask to come into this world. God didn't consult us as to when we should be born. We are not responsible for our birthdate, nor are we responsible for our exit. We are not responsible for the way we came in; we will be held accountable and responsible for the way we go out. We did not ask to be born into the life or the family or the home into which we were born. We did not ask to be born with sinful natures. We did not have a choice in the matter, but I do believe that God does not make any mistakes.

I want to continue to expound on biblical truths that will keep us moving forward. The Christian race is not a sprint race, it's more of a long distance race into eternity.

We did not ask to exist at all. God did not consult us when He planned for our lives in this world. God has a plan for you, and God has a plan for me. One thing is sure: though we were born in sin, He did not intend for us to leave this world in a sinful state but that we should live in peace with Him and without spot and blameless before Him, that we may enjoy His wonderful heaven, the place He has prepared for those who love him.

I want to share my testimony because as I stated in Chapter 3 of the last book, my race was almost over, but God saw fit to rescue me just in the nick of time. I have lived a life of sin. Any sin disqualifies us from the race. It doesn't matter what church you belong to or how long you have been in church. As soon as you enter into your sin nature, you are disqualified. However, God loves the sinner but he doesn't love the sin.

It took me a while to figure out my purpose. The true statement is all things work together for good for those who love God. Many people are entering into this Christian race daily and yes, there are some that have been disqualified. I pray that this writing will encourage you on the discipline that it takes to be a Christian athlete. As an athlete, we have to get in shape for our destiny.

I am committed and submitted to something greater than myself.

Back in April 2016, the Lord was down on me regarding my health. As I stated before, I was 279 pounds and prescribed two different types of high blood pressure medications. God spoke to me in many ways as I traveled to find rest in Cozumel, Mexico. He began to speak to me through my wife.

A lot of times, we know that we are out of shape but God will speak through the ones we love because sometimes we won't listen until it becomes too much. After my trip, I decided to start walking. I started with one mile per day and now I am walking 5-7 miles per day and 10 miles on the weekends. I have always been athletic, but I allowed myself to get out of shape physically and spiritually.

I remember way back in junior high when I first started practicing football. A great friend of mind by the name of Richie Garrett was there for me when I came to the Avondale school system. As you read in the last book, I was way out of shape spiritually as well as physically because I had a heavy drinking problem. If it had not been for Richie's encouragement, I probably would've flunked out of that school system as well because of my sin.
I was calling "Earl!" in a trash can on the side of the building one day after binge drinking liquor the night before. That was an indicator that something had seriously gotten a hold of me.

It took me a little while to get in shape. It was the coaching staff, the physical activity, and also my teammates that God placed in my life that were my inspiration. During 1979 through 1983 and beyond I really didn't understand my purpose. That's why I was caught up in the trials of life.

The Preliminaries of life is where you make all your mistakes. The Semi-Finals is where you begin to get things right. But you still can be disqualified. I would like to state that the Finals is where you reach your destination.

There are only two places that the road of life will lead you - to heaven or hell.

I would like to share with you this paradigm: Just imagine that you driving alone down a country road. The sun is shining, the scenery is spectacular, the flowers are blooming, and the grass is evergreen. You get to the hillside country which is where the Spirit of the Lord begins to deal with you about the road you are traveling. While driving, a church on a hill catches your eye. The Spirit of God has drawn you to this church. You get out of your car, proceed to the entrance of the church, walk in, and notice that it is packed with familiar people. You walk down the aisle because all the seats in back are full. You proceed to the front and as you do, you notice your closest family members are sitting there.

As you look around, you notice friends, coworkers, and neighbors adorning the pews. The music starts playing and it is then you then you turn your eyes to the front of the altar area and you see a casket. You approach the casket then you look down in the casket and you see yourself.

My question to you as you read this book entitled finish strong: "What will your eulogy be like? What will your family say about you? Did you leave a legacy for your children? What will your pastor say in the eulogy, where will you spend eternity? Will you be disqualified? Will you make it to the Finals? What is your final destination? Is in heaven or is it hell?

Chapter 1
The Preliminaries

I would like to define the Preliminaries as the entry-level. It is where a lot of mistakes are being made. We can enter live haphazardly without instruction or heed the warnings that may cost our life as well as our soul. God inspired great prophets in the Bible to lead his people to victory.

Let us look at what the Bible says. The Prophet Ezekiel sounded one of the early warnings against a man's spiritual defeat.

WHEN A RIGHTEOUS MAN DIES IN INIQUITY

"When a righteous man turneth away from his righteousness, and committeth iniquity, and dieth in them; for his iniquity that he hath done shall he die." Ezekiel 18:26

You may live many years in righteousness, but if you return to your sins, you will die in your sins. We have to stay in the right relationship with God.

We can disqualify ourselves.

Galatians 5:7 - You did run will what hinder you? You were doing so well. Who stopped you from being influenced by the truth?

YOU MUST ABIDE IN THE VINE, OR BE CUT OFF, CAST OUT, BURNED

Everything we get from the word of God will condition us for the Finals of life.

Everyone has an opportunity to get in shape for the kingdom of heaven but the fact is everyone is not qualified. In my last book "From Sin & Shame to Glory", I took you on a journey through the five lanes of life.

Lane One was the fact of sin. Lane Two was the fact of separation. Lane Three was the ultimate judgment and Lane Four was the fact of redemption. The Victory Lane is the closest to heaven.

I almost died in Lane Three but by God's grace, I was put back on the field to continue in the race of life. In this book I will only focus on three chapters that will get you to victory. Let us proceed to prepare our spirits for the instructions onto righteousness, the right way of doing things.

The Bible states:

Matthew 22:29 - There is a way that seem right, but the end there of is destruction.

We error from two things: not knowing the scripture or the power of God.

"Do it for the Vine" is an expression used to urge someone to perform a dare on camera for a Vine video. It became a well-known catchphrase within the community after a video clip of a little girl dancing to the chant went viral on the vide-sharing platform. I believe we need to do it for Jesus.

The Holy Spirit has already gone viral getting into the heart in the spirit of many believers.

Jesus said,
John 15:1-3 - "I am the true vine, and my Father is the husbandman. Every branch in me that beareth not fruit he taketh away: and every branch that beareth fruit, he purgeth it, that it may bring forth more fruit. Now ye are clean through the word which I have spoken unto you.

We can fall back to our old ways. A backsliders' heart is filled with its old ways. I can recall the times that I relapsed and fell out of the will of God. It was because I didn't apply myself spiritually and I set myself up for setback. We can get caught up in the moment around people, places, and things. We can get complacent, lazy, nonchalant, and ignorant to spiritual principles.

We must remember just going to church doesn't save us. No matter what church you go to, if you don't have a personal relationship with Jesus Christ you will fall from grace. I personally don't believe "once saved, always saved" because we can go through the motions and still miss God.

Jesus said,
John 15:4-6 - Abide in me, and I in you. As the branch cannot bear fruit of itself, except it abide in the vine; no more can ye, except ye abide in me. I am the vine, ye are the branches: He that abideth in me, and I in him, the same bringeth forth much fruit: for without me ye can do nothing. If a man abide not in me, he is cast forth as a branch, and is withered; and men gather them, and cast them into the fire, and they are burned."

Many people have died at an early age, and many of them were disqualified. Some people learn from their mistakes and some go down because the **wages of sin is death** and the gift of God is eternal life. But if we abide in the word of God we shall live.

I don't think it is possible to be any plainer. If you do not stay in Christ and in His Word, you will be cut off and cast out. You will die and be destroyed. That is not eternal security.

That is not "once-saved, always-saved". We can become self-righteous. We can develop an independent spirit, we can easily adapt to a religious spirit.

Religion won't get us in heaven. In fact, if our religion doesn't change us, we need to change our religion. It is more than going to church. We must become the church. Know that your body is the temple of God in as the Spirit of God that wells down inside of you.

Nobody in their right mind would go into a church and go to the trashcan and empty out all the trash in the midst of the church; yet, we still trash our temples, our bodies, by putting drugs and alcohol and pornography in. Foul words come out of the heart through our mouth. We come to church and leave church the same away. Time in and time out we struggle until we decide that we need to enter in a total commitment to Christ. So it is in the natural, it shall be also in the spirit. We need to discipline ourselves. We need to write activity, we need mentors, we need coaches but most importantly we need to make an effort to be all we can be.

As long as you know you are in and have done the will of God...keep it moving! Don't be distracted by opposition. Keep it moving forward!

GETTING INTO CONDITION

I would like to stress the importance of spiritual condition. I think you understand the concept about physical condition. If you don't take care of your body you would not perform well. Your body will let you know. The pain will come; the strain, aches and fatigue will come. You will get burnt out if you're not properly conditioned.

With that being said, you have to build up your endurance. Spiritually, we need to start conditioning ourselves with confession; because, confession is made unto salvation. Salvation is what Jesus did for us on Calvary. We just don't join a church. We have to be born into the church.

We all have been prodigal, spending money or resources freely and recklessly. It's wasteful, extravagant living. If I could get back just half of the money that I smoked up in crack cocaine, drank in alcohol, spent at the bars, I would be a rich man. My riotous prodigal living was a waste.

If only I had back the years in lost in relationships.

By now you know my story, but I am here to help you get through the highs and lows of life. There will be times that you really don't feel like carrying on. There will be times when you are not motivated. There will be times when it seems like the whole world is upon your shoulders. These are the times we need listen to the Holy Spirit.

After getting saved, God promises us the Comforter, which will come alongside to help us with life's struggles. Yes, we make poor choices and mistakes from time to time.

The Preliminaries are there to show you that you don't have it all together and that you are weak and in your weakness, you will fail. Now that you understand, you need to make up your mind to welcome that coach into your life, welcome the parents, teachers, and spiritual fathers. You need discipline and endurance because the difficulties of life will come.

We will be confronted with opposition, spiritual warfare, adversity, controversy, and whatever the world has to offer. We cannot hide from our troubles, but we can learn how to live a life in Christ Jesus. We can capitalize on our mistakes, we can train ourselves to live in the will of God, and we can live life more abundantly through his Word.

What's in your spirit when you are losing?

Ok, now what if the negativity is coming from INSIDE of you? Let's say you came into the race with confidence and enthusiasm, but your opponent or opposing team is just better, stronger, faster, and wiser? You begin to get frustrated, lose your focus, your mind races with negative thoughts, and you don't even want to keep going because you KNOW you are not going to win.

If that happens, here's what I recommend:

1. Switch your focus away from the outcome.

Why are you here? If it's only for the glory of winning then you might as well never participate again because losing is just a natural part of sports, period. YOU ARE GOING TO LOSE. Say it with me, "I AM GOING TO LOSE SOMETIMES." The quicker you understand this, the quicker you will be able to connect with the true heart of what you are doing.

So why are you here, doing this and playing this game or performing in this sport? I would imagine it's because you just love it, because it is fun and challenging, and it pushes you to new heights physically, mentally, and emotionally. Well, if that's the case then there's no reason that it can't happen when you're losing! If you take the end goal of winning for the sake of winning off the table then you are left with fun, stretching your skills, and learning about what you can work on to improve next time. When you put it that way then LOSING sounds like another form of winning to me!

2. Concentrate on the action, not your thoughts.

A very common occurrence in the midst of a losing performance is negative thoughts like, "How could I have messed up like that", "I suck at this, I should just quit right now", or, "I'll never be as good as him/her". These thoughts don't just stay in your mind, they cause your muscles to tighten, your attention to move away from the action, and are very likely to hurt your performance even further than if you just made a mistake and quickly rebounded by staying connected with what's happening around you.

So if that happens, just brush those thoughts aside in the moment and bring your attention back to your breathing, to the position of the ball or the beam, to staying alert and ready to move your body wherever it needs to go. Tell yourself that if you really want to, you'll have time to think later, but for now just **stay in the game**. The mental energy you're NOT WASTING on negative thoughts can instead be applied to your performance and help you close the margin of loss, even if you still don't win.

3.   Practice more.

Athletes who take practice seriously, challenge themselves to continually improve, and accept **good coaching** will always perform better than those who don't. If the reason you find yourself on the losing side is due to a lack of preparedness or insufficient practice, then take this loss as valuable motivation to reinvest yourself in practice.

Maybe you need to practice more often, maybe it's a matter of improving your **concentration**, or maybe it's time to get a better trainer who is more aligned with your vision and goals. Rather than dwelling on the loss of this performance, use it to create a new game plan for how you'll maximize your practice time going forward.

One note here though: NEVER push yourself harder than your body is ready to stretch, never play or practice through injuries, and always take good care of yourself. **Are you coachable?**

You Are Further Along Than You Think

Let me invite you into the true reality that you are actually further along than you think. The race is in the bag! You're in Christ and Christ is already at the finish line. You can't lose! The enemy knows this and so his only move is to try to make you more tired, more disappointed, more offended that you aren't further along. He will try to get you so discouraged that you stop running altogether.

The Father wants you to know that He is running this with you. That it may feel like you're not as far as you want to be, but it's probably because you've never run this part of the race before. You've never been where you are right now. Of course it seems a little foreign. But you're closer than you think. So be encouraged, run with purpose and confidence. The Father is great at setting the perfect pace for your victory.

There's another word for teachability: HUMILITY.

Chapter 2
The Semi Finals

I would like to define the Semi-Finals, where you have discovered your mistakes and now you realize your strengths and your weaknesses. At this point you had some agonies in some defeat. The question is, will you advance to the next level?

I would always capitalize on the next day to try to achieve more. I would like to compare the similarities to the spiritual realm. God has blessed me to finish my first book "From Sin & Shame to Glory" after having this book in my heart for many years.

God wants us to strive toward excellence. God wants us to be determined to achieve in spite of life's difficulties and in spite of adversity. If we take the time to condition ourselves spiritually, we will find that we reach spiritual results. We will have a stronger Christian mentally, mind, body, and soul.

Physically, we will be able to endure the rigorous routines of life. It takes a made-up mind. It takes an individual challenging themselves. So spiritually I love feeling good about myself and also looking good to encourage myself.

I do get a lot of compliments, but at the end of the day, I represent the Kingdom of God and I have to feel good about myself. I cannot let myself go down. I cannot let myself get out of shape. I cannot afford to just not do anything.

I reaped a blessing from my efforts when I visited my doctor recently. For over ten years the doctor had prescribed me high blood pressure medicine to help keep my pressure down. It had gotten so bad at one point that he prescribed me two prescriptions at one time. But because of my efforts of walking and conditioning and eating right, I am no longer on medication. The Semi-Finals is where you realize that you have the potential to be all you can be. It is in the Semi-Finals where you begin to quote the scripture, "I can do all things through Christ who strengthens me". It is in the Semi-Finals where you develop the right mindset, a sense of accomplishment, and you can smell victory.

Continue to be out you can be you can make it to the Finals!

THE SCHOOL OF DEFEAT

The prodigal son would have been lost if he had not returned to the Father and repented.

The prodigal son was running the race at one time in his life, but he took his eyes off the prize of his high calling. He began to look back into the world and he was carried away by the lust of his flesh. He thought the grass was greener on the other side. He wanted to run in the fast lane. He sprinted towards the nightlife in a foreign country. He wasted his inheritance in worldly living, only to come back home to his father, his coach, who accepted him back on his team.

In Luke 15, Jesus taught that the Prodigal Son left his father and "wasted his substance on riotous living." Finding himself in great want, he said, "I will arise and go to my father, and will say unto him, Father, I have sinned against heaven, and before thee, and am no more worthy to be called thy son: make me as one of thy hired servants."

When he returned to his FATHER, his father welcomed him saying, "For this **my son was dead**, and is alive again; he was lost, and is found. And they began to be merry," Luke 15:18-24.

If the Prodigal Son Had not returned to his FATHER and REPENTED, he would have been lost.

I WILL REMOVE THY CANDLESTICK

The Holy Ghost warned backsliders in the Church at Ephesus to "**REPENT, and do the first works**, or else I will come unto thee quickly, and will **remove thy candlestick** out of his place, except thou repent," Revelation 2:5.

This requires that they actually have a candlestick in the Church. This prophecy would be discussion if those saints had not actually been a candlestick in the Kingdom of God.

Proverbs 20:27 - The spirit of man is the candle of the LORD, searching all the inward parts of the belly.

That means that even though you may be In the Body of Christ, the Church today, God may remove (disqualify) you from the Church if you have unrepented sins.

BLOTTED OUT OF THE BOOK OF LIFE= BEING DISQUALIFIED

Revelation 3:5 - To him that overcometh, the Spirit says, "I will not blot his name out of the book of life".

If you don't overcome the world, the flesh and the devil, your name will be disqualified or blotted out. That presumes that your name was actually in the Book of Life but now you have violated the rules, you step out of the will of God, you missed the mark.

Your name may be in the Book of Life today, but if you go to the Judgment with unrepented sins, you will find that your name has been blotted out.

TAKE AWAY HIS PART OUT OF THE BOOK OF LIFE

Revelation 22:19 - If any man shall take away from the words of the book of this prophecy, God shall take away his part out of the book of life, and out of the holy city.

Your name cannot be taken out of a book that it is not in. This prophecy could only be true if their names had actually been in the Book of Life.

Revelation 20:12-14a - And I saw the dead, small and great, stand before God; and the books were opened: and another book was opened, which is the book of life: and the dead were judged out of those things which were written in the books, according to their works. And the sea gave up the dead which were in it; and death and hell delivered up the dead which were in them: and they were judged every man according to their works. And death and hell were cast into the lake of fire. This is the second death. And whosoever was not found written in the book of life was cast into the lake of fire.

Again, your name may be in the Book of Life right now, but if you take away from the words of this book of prophecy (if you teach or preach against the Truth of the Word of God), your name will be "taken away" from the Book of Life on Judgment Day.

REMOVED FROM HIM THAT CALLED YOU

Sometime we move out of position and jump timing. We jumped the gun, soon to be disqualified in the tribulation of this life.

Don't allow anything or anyone to move you out of position. Stay where you are planted. This is no season to church hop. Many people are so quick to leave their local church when they have been corrected, reproved, and chastised because of some action that disqualifies them from moving forward in life.

It can be an act of the adultery. Any relapse into any type of sin can simply be just a disobedient spirit.

THE LITTLE FOXES

Song 2:15 - Take us the foxes, the little foxes, that spoil the vines: for our vines have tender grapes.

- Small things trip us up
- The small little lies
- Misunderstanding that follows instruction
- Crossing into someone else's lane

What's moving in this season?

Most American churchgoers are hearing about the issue of issues at their places of worship. But most say their ministers are not taking a position for or against the true holiness, and relatively few people say their own views on the issue are being shaped by religious leaders or their own religious beliefs. It is making a major impact, because our land is sick with moral decay.

2 Timothy 3:1-5 - This know also, that in the last days perilous times shall come.
2 For men shall be lovers of their own selves, covetous, boasters, proud, blasphemers, disobedient to parents, unthankful, unholy, 3 Without natural affection, trucebreakers, false accusers, incontinent, fierce, despisers of those that are good, 4 Traitors, heady, highminded, lovers of pleasures more than lovers of God; 5 Having a form of godliness, but denying the power thereof: from such turn away.

Have nothing to do with such people. These things move people from the grace of God.

Galatians 1:6-8 - I marvel that ye are so soon removed from him that called you into the grace of Christ unto another gospel: Which is not another; but there be some that trouble you, and would pervert the gospel of Christ. But though we, or an angel from heaven, preach any other gospel unto you than that which we have preached unto you, let him be accursed.
There is a lot of preaching but is it sound doctrine?

What exactly does it mean to be "removed from Him that called you"? First of all, HE DID CALL YOU. You may have even been CHOSEN. But you weren't FAITHFUL. You followed a false gospel, and now you have been **removed from Him that called you...** Removed from God!

This is a horrible warning that AFTER HAVING BEEN CALLED OF GOD, we can be "removed from God." If you turn from the true Gospel to a false gospel, you are turning from God. You are removed from God.

Protocol: a system of rules that explain the correct conduct and procedures to be followed in formal situations.

We can step out of line of kingdom protocol, God's word. God give us instruction on how to run the Christian race. We can be unfit for the kingdom of God if we look back to our worldly lust.

Luke 9:52 - And Jesus said unto him, No man, having put his hand to the plough, and looking back, is fit for the kingdom of God.

Jude 1:18-19 - ...they told you there should be mockers in the last time, who should walk after their own ungodly lusts. These be they who separate themselves.

Isaiah 59:2 - ...your iniquities have separated between you and your God, and your sins have hid his face from you, that he will not hear.

BUILDING UP YOUR ENDURANCE.

Endurance: the fact or power of enduring an unpleasant or difficult process or situation
CASTAWAY

The great Apostle Paul said,

1 Corinthians 9:27 - "I keep under my body, and bring it into subjection: lest that by any means, when I have preached to others, I myself should be a castaway,"

Castaway = "REJECTED, UNAPPROVED."

Paul was a confirmed Apostle, at legitimate RISK of being REJECTED and UNAPPROVED by God if he did not keep his body in subjection to the Spirit.

If the Apostle Paul was concerned about becoming a CASTAWAY, then I believe that you and I should also be concerned, and take every precaution not to become a CASTAWAY.

If you refuse to keep your body under subjection to the will of God, you will become a CASTAWAY - a reject, unapproved in jeopardy of being disqualified.

THE HEALTHY AGE OF COMPETITION

As I transferred into the Avondale school system in 1978 I learned to appreciate culture. I began healthy friendships. Even though I was very quiet, I had a lot going on in my mind at that time. I have some regrets and I often say if I had it to do over again I would've made better choices.

While attending school and working at such a young age, I soon realized I had no spiritual discipline. That is a requirement along with growing in relationship with God. There were several highlights of my life where I missed the mark.

Be aware of competitiveness that leads to jealousy. Canes competitiveness towards his brother, Abel, led him to murder.

Genesis 4:1-8 - And Adam knew Eve his wife; and she conceived, and bare Cain, and said, I have gotten a man from the LORD.

2 And she again bare his brother Abel. And Abel was a keeper of sheep, but Cain was a tiller of the ground.

3 And in process of time it came to pass, that Cain brought of the fruit of the ground an offering unto the LORD.

4 And Abel, he also brought of the firstlings of his flock and of the fat thereof. And the LORD had respect unto Abel and to his offering:

5 But unto Cain and to his offering he had not respect. And Cain was very wroth, and his countenance fell.

6 And the LORD said unto Cain, Why art thou wroth? and why is thy countenance fallen?

7 If thou doest well, shalt thou not be accepted? and if thou doest not well, sin lieth at the door. And unto thee shall be his desire, and thou shalt rule over him.

8 And Cain talked with Abel his brother: and it came to pass, when they were in the field, that Cain rose up against Abel his brother, and slew him.

He tried to put his brother down in order to lift himself up.

Saul also tried to kill David. When the crowd sang, "Saul have slain his thousand, and David his 10,000"

1 Samuel 18:6-11 - And it came to pass as they came, when David was returned from the slaughter of the Philistine, that the women came out of all cities of Israel, singing and dancing, to meet king Saul, with tabrets, with joy, and with instruments of musick.
7 And the women answered one another as they played, and said, Saul hath slain his thousands, and David his ten thousands.
8 And Saul was very wroth, and the saying displeased him; and he said, They have ascribed unto David ten thousands, and to me they have ascribed but thousands: and what can he have more but the kingdom?
9 And Saul eyed David from that day and forward.
10 And it came to pass on the morrow, that the evil spirit from God came upon Saul, and he prophesied in the midst of the house: and David played with his hand, as at other times: and there was a javelin in Saul's hand.
11 And Saul cast the javelin; for he said, I will smite David even to the wall with it. And David avoided out of his presence twice.

Those words caused jealousy to grow. We must understand that by seeking to excel in our calling, we must exalt Christ.

Paul writes:

1 Corinthians 9:24-25 – Know ye not that they which run in a race run all, but one receiveth the prize? So run, that ye may obtain.
25 And every man that striveth for the mastery is temperate in all things. Now they do it to obtain a corruptible crown; but we an incorruptible.

There is no second grade effort, no 70 for mediocrity, and no time for complacency. I am running hard to the finish line. I may not be the best father or the best Pastor or the best Christian but my mentality is this: I'm going to give my best every time, even if I don't start on the team. I'm still going to practice. I'm still going to give my best effort when I get in the game. I'm still going try to the Finish Line.

I would like to encourage you to do your very best and once you give your best, God will do the rest. God is changing the individual, God is touching the man's heart. Once He touches a man, the man then goes home to encourage his wife. His children are blessed because of his position in Christ.

Now, there is a blessed family. The blessed family goes to the church in their neighborhood, joins the church, and now the church is blessed because of their commitment. Churches are full of blessed men and women of God who decided to make a commitment to that church in their city. This what makes their state great. This is what it's going to make America great. It's not going to be a politician. It is going to be because we all are Christians and now we have entered this race and we are better together.

Winning isn't everything. We must understand we win some and we lose some. Our culture needs to understand that what makes this great again is seeking first the Kingdom of God. So don't be disappointed at failure just get up, dust yourself off, and get back on the track.

Get prepared physically, spiritually, and mentally that you will not become disqualified.

THEY KNEW GOD, BUT GOD GAVE THEM OVER TO A REPROBATE MIND

Paul spoke of men who KNEW GOD.

Romans 1:21, 28 - Because that, when **they knew** *God, they glorified him not as God, neither were thankful; but became vain in their imaginations, and their foolish heart was darkened.*

And even as they did not like to RETAIN GOD in their knowledge, God gave them over to a reprobate mind.

They did not BEGIN with a reprobate mind. God gave it to them because of their **rejection** of Him.

A reprobate mind no longer calls good good, or evil, evil. It calls good evil and evil good. I don't want to characterize specific Sins because God loves the person but He **hates the Sin**.

You may KNOW GOD TODAY, but if you do not GLORIFY HIM AS GOD, if you become unthankful, or vain in your imagination so that your heart becomes darkened, God will GIVE YOU OVER to a REPROBATE MIND.

You will become a REPROBATE, calling good evil and evil good.

That is a CONDEMNED state. We all have been there before and that's not a good place.

THEY HAD FAITH, BUT MADE SHIPWRECK

1 Timothy 1:19 - Holding faith, and a good conscience; which some having put away concerning faith have made shipwreck.

A ship that is wrecked does not reach its intended destination. But this also presumes that you were in fact IN THE SHIP.

We can lose fellowship with our family, with our friends, we can isolate ourselves, and get connected with the bad a cloud of witnesses. We have a free will of choice.

You may HAVE FAITH TODAY, and you may HAVE A GOOD CONSCIENCE, but if you PUT AWAY YOUR FAITH, or PUT AWAY YOUR GOOD CONSCIENCE, you will make SHIPWRECK.

My ship was wrecked when I was drinking and smoking crack cocaine. My ship was wrecked when I was looking at pornography. My ship was wrecked when I thought I could do it by myself. My whole family's ship was in jeopardy to wreck because of my disobedience to God.

Is it really necessary for me to explain that shipwrecks SINK into the abyss and are never seen or heard from again? I mentioned to you in the third Chapter of my last book, my ship was sinking in Gulfport Mississippi, the devil had come to kill, steal, and destroy. But God rescued me in order for me to write this book and to coach His people into their destinies.

If today was your last day where will you spend eternity?

The world is full of darkness. The world is full of agony and defeat. We are the children of light and therefore, we should understand that there is a difference between light and dark.

If we don't live right, we will lose our privileges and positions in the Christian race. We will be given a bad lane assignment. We will have a poor time due to our own hidden agendas and we will lose our position in Christ.

CHILDREN OF THE KINGDOM CAST INTO OUTER DARKNESS

Matthew 8:12 - But the children of the kingdom shall be cast out into outer darkness: there shall be weeping and gnashing of teeth.

Yes, this is a hard saying, but there will be "children of the kingdom" in Hell. They were born again, but they failed in the end. Sons of God in Hell.

You may have been A CHILD OF THE KINGDOM at some point in your life, but if you succumb to doubt, fear and unbelief, you will be cast into outer darkness, where there will be weeping and gnashing of teeth.

Have you ever made a mistake so big that it made you scream or cry in painful regret? If so, multiply that by millions. That will be Hell. Death is final. Salvation is Eternal in heaven "as well as hell."

No matter what JOYS you may have experienced with God on earth, if you forsake Him, you will spend eternity in painful regrets in Hell.

SPUED OUT OF HIS MOUTH.

Revelation 3:16 - So then because thou art lukewarm, and neither cold nor hot, I will spue thee out of my mouth.
Again, the word is very clear. It stands to reason that if you were not in His mouth, you would not have been spewed out.

How can anyone fail to see that Jesus gives a clear warning here: "Do not become lukewarm! I will spew you out!"

CALLED, CHOSEN, AND FAITHFUL

Revelation 17:14 - These shall make war with the Lamb, and the Lamb shall overcome them: for he is Lord of lords, and King of kings: and they that are with him are called, and chosen, and faithful.

These were not only CALLED, but CHOSEN. It is not good enough to be CALLED. Many are CALLED, but few are CHOSEN. But neither is it good enough to be CHOSEN. We must be FAITHFUL. Consistent and dedicated to the word of God.

If we want to hear Jesus say, "Well done, thou good and faithful servant," we must in fact be a good and FAITHFUL SERVANT.

If you are not GOOD and FAITHFUL, you will NOT hear, "Well done."

DEMAS HATH FORSAKEN, HAVING LOVED THIS PRESENT WORLD

2 Timothy 4:10 - For Demas hath forsaken me, having loved this present world, and is departed...

Demas had been a fellow minister with Paul, Luke, Judas and many others. They had been called and chosen, but he did not make his election sure.

I can include my name to this list because there were times when I wasn't good and faithful. There was also many things that hindered me in my Christian race. The Bible states:

Galatians 5:7 - You did run will but what hindered you that you would not obey the truth.

Who hindered you? What stopped you from moving forward? What caused you to fall back in sin? Why did you relapse? Why did you not obey the truth? Why did you choose wrong when God's word showed you what was right?

If you LOVE THIS PRESENT WORLD, be afraid. The world will lead us astray. We will depart and we will forsake so, turn back!

MAKE YOUR CALLING AND ELECTION SURE

I entered into the race in 1993. I was disqualified up to that point. I needed Jesus as my Lord and Savior. I was running out of control. My life was dysfunctional. I needed the Holy Spirit to be my guide and I needed a spiritual coach. I HAD to surrender.

Your success is in your surrender. We have to come clean or stay away nasty. I discovered, mostly through trial and error, about the slips, trips, and falls and how to get back up and run the race.

All of Heaven is Cheering You On! STAY IN THE GAME!

In 1995, I answered the call of ministry. I can recall that summer, my Dad was diagnosed with a terminal illness. He had throat cancer. The Spirit of the Lord was dealing with me in our church services. I was following my Pastor, and he was following Christ. I was dedicated to his vision and I prayed for him and loved him like my own father.

The congregation welcomed my wife and me with open arms. The worship was amazing and we sang songs like, "Victory is Mine", "I Have Put on the Garment of Praise", "Can't Nobody Do Me Like Jesus" and "I Was Glad When They Said Unto Me Let Us Go Into The House Of The Lord". There was one song in particular. That was a song by Sister Maria Johnson, "He Meant to for My Good".

That song brought deliverance to my life. As you read in my last book, "From Sin and Shame to Glory", I wasn't fit until God came into my life. I looked forward to coming to church. It didn't matter what position I held, all I needed was deliverance.

Yes, I was shy at first, but in the midst of the Holy Spirit I would praise God like I had lost my mind. I believe God was getting me ready for this race. There is one song says that he is preparing me.

In 1997, I started pastoring a church that taught me how to be a coach. I am still in this race, after 23 years, 19 of which I spent as a spiritual coach. I made my calling and election sure.

I almost forgot to add the most important moment in my Christian race. It was a Sunday after church driving back to Picayune, Mississippi on I-59. I was passing the Millard exit and the Spirit of the Lord filled me with the precious Holy Ghost. I had to pull over because I was overcome with the unknown tongues as the Spirit gave me utterance. This was a moment of empowerment. This was the fulfillment of God's promise. This was a free gift that He is willing to give all believers. This is why I am still running today. It is for the power of the Holy Spirit.

2 Peter 1:10 - *Wherefore the rather, brethren, give diligence to make your calling and election sure: for if ye do these things, ye shall never fall.*

Your CALLING and ELECTION is NOT sure if you are not DILIGENT to MAKE IT SURE. I you don't continue the path of righteousness you can lead others to be disqualified.

It is UP TO YOU to live for God. There is no "eternal security" for any Christian who returns to their sins. Nobody is ONCE-SAVED, ALWAYS-SAVED until they rise up in the First Resurrection and Rapture of the saints.

OUR LAMPS ARE GONE OUT

Matthew 25:8 - *And the foolish [virgins] said unto the wise, Give us of your oil; for our lamps are gone out.*

There had been LIGHT in their LAMPS, but they went out. They were born of the Spirit, but they did not keep the fire of the Spirit burning through prayer and a consecrated life. When the Bridegroom comes, you will be left behind, as they were.

THE UNPROFITABLE SERVANT CAST OUT

Matthew 25:30 - And cast ye the unprofitable servant into outer darkness: there shall be weeping and gnashing of teeth.

Those who were profitable entered into the joy of their LORD.

If you are UNPROFITABLE, you will be cast out.
SALT THAT LOSES ITS SAVOR IS CAST OUT

Matthew 5:13 - Ye are the salt of the earth: but if the salt have lost his savour, wherewith shall it be salted? It is thenceforth good for nothing, but to be cast out, and to be trodden under foot of men.

They WERE the Salt of the earth, but they lost their value and purpose.

If you lose your savor, your godliness, your holiness, you will be cast out.

TAKE HEED LEST HE SPARE NOT THEE

Romans 11:21 - For if God spared not the natural branches, take heed lest he also spare not thee.

If God cut off Jews who were apostate, He can and will also cut off Christians who are apostate.

CUT OFF FOR NOT CONTINUING

Romans 11:22 - Behold therefore the goodness and severity of God: on them which fell, severity; but toward thee, goodness, if thou continue in his goodness: otherwise thou also shalt be cut off.

Be careful not to provoke the wrath - the severity - of God, by disobedient living. If you do, "thou also shalt be CUT OFF."

"FAIL OF THE GRACE OF GOD," THEREBY BE DEFILED

Hebrews 12:15 - Looking diligently lest any man fail of the grace of God; lest any root of bitterness springing up trouble you, and thereby many be defiled.

If you FAIL (fall short of) the grace of God, that means you fall from His favor. If you fall from God's favor, "thereby many be defiled [tainted, contaminated]."

PLUCKED OUT? OR, JUMPED OUT?

John 10:28 - Jesus said, "My sheep hear my voice, and I know them, and they follow me: And I give unto them eternal life; and they shall never perish, neither shall any man pluck them out of my hand".

Jesus made this promise, "No man can pluck them out of my hand, because **THEY FOLLOW ME.**" But if you do not **FOLLOW HIM**, you are not IN His hand.

Hebrews 13:5 - He hath said, I will never leave thee, nor forsake thee.

Notwithstanding, although HE will not LEAVE YOU, if YOU LEAVE HIM, He will not force His relationship with you. He will leave you to your devices.

2 Chronicles 15:2 - The LORD is with you, while ye be with him; and if ye seek him, he will be found of you; but if ye forsake him, he will forsake you.

INIQUITIES SEPARATE YOU FROM GOD. HE HIDES HIS FACE.

Isaiah 59:2- Your iniquities have separated between you and your God, and your sins have hid his face from you, that he will not hear.

Nobody can take you OUT of His hand if you are IN it. But if you get OUT of His hand because your SINS SEPARATE you from His hand, you are NOT secure. There is a PREMIUM on FAITHFULNESS, and a PENALTY for UNFAITHFULNESS.

HE THAT LOOKS BACK IS UNFIT

Luke 9:62 - Jesus said unto him, No man, having put his hand to the plough, and looking back, is fit for the kingdom of God.

Luke 17:32 - ...he that is in the field, let him likewise not return back. Remember Lot's wife.

REMEMBER LOT'S WIFE

Genesis 19:17 - When the Angel of the Lord delivered her, he said, "Escape for thy life; look not behind thee, ...lest thou be consumed".

Tragically, she DID look back.

Genesis 19:26 - But his wife looked back from behind him, and she became a pillar of salt.

REQUIRED TO BE FAITHFUL

1 Corinthians 4:2 - Moreover it is required in stewards, that a man be found faithful.

Revelation 2:10 - Be thou faithful unto death, and I will give thee a crown of life.

BOTH of these verses clearly insinuate that if I am NOT faithful unto death, I will NOT receive a crown of life.

Matthew 10:39 - Jesus said, "He that FINDETH his life shall lose it."

Matthew 16:25 - Jesus said, "He that SAVETH his life shall lose it."

So, if you GET WHAT YOU WANT down here, you WON'T get what He has up there.
IF WE HOLD THE BEGINNING OF OUR CONFIDENCE STEDFAST UNTO THE END

Hebrews 3:14 - For we are made partakers of Christ, if we hold the beginning of our confidence steadfast unto the end.

Therefore, be warned!

2 Peter 3:17 - Ye therefore, beloved, seeing ye know these things before, BEWARE LEST YE ALSO, being led away with the error of the wicked, FALL FROM YOUR OWN STEDFASTNESS.

Why would Peter WARN us not to fall from our steadfastness if we are once-saved, always-saved?

Hebrews 10:35 - Cast not away therefore your confidence, which hath great recompence of reward.

If you do cast away your confidence, there is no promise of "great recompence of reward."

2 Peter 2:4,20-22 - For if God spared not the angels that sinned, but cast them down to hell, and delivered them into chains of darkness, to be reserved unto judgment; ...if after they have escaped the pollutions of the world through the knowledge of the Lord and Saviour Jesus Christ, they are again entangled therein, and overcome, the latter end is worse with them than the beginning.

For it had been better for them not to have known the way of righteousness, than, after they have known it, to turn from the holy commandment delivered unto them. But it is happened unto them according to the true proverb, the dog is turned to his own vomit again; and the sow that was washed to her wallowing in the mire.

James 1:15 - When lust hath conceived, it bringeth forth sin: and sin, when it is finished, bringeth forth death.

- Spiritual death
- Spiritual burn out
- Drawn away by your own lust

Matthew 10:22 - ...but he that endureth to the end shall be saved.

IF YE KEEP MY COMMANDMENTS

Jesus said that the REASON the Father loved Him is because HE KEPT HIS FATHER'S COMMANDMENTS or kept His words. We have to do what He says in order to get what He has.

John 15:10 - If ye keep my commandments, ye shall abide in my love; even as I have kept my Father's commandments, and abide in his love.

The underlying reality in His statement is that if you DO NOT KEEP COMMANDMENTS, you will NOT abide in the love of God. Any less a conclusion is simply a denial of the fact. You had better get started right now keeping the commandments of God if you want to abide in the love of God. Jesus said it.

If you don't STUDY the Word of God, and KNOW the commandments of God, you are in big trouble.

BACKSLIDING IS A BIBLICAL TERM

- "Backsliding Israel," Jeremiah 3:6,8,11-12.
- "Backsliding children," Jeremiah 3:14,22.
- "People of Jerusalem ...backsliding," Jeremiah 8:5.
- "Backsliding daughter," Jeremiah 31:22; 49:4.
- "Israel slideth back as a backsliding heifer," Hosea 4:16.
- "My people are bent to backsliding from me," Hosea 11:7.

Hosea 14:1-4- O Israel, return unto the LORD thy God; for thou hast fallen by thine iniquity. Take with you words, and turn to the LORD: say unto him, Take away all iniquity, and receive us graciously: ...I will heal their backsliding, I will love them freely: for mine anger is turned away...

God warned Israel to return and repent, and He would heal their backsliding and turn away His anger.

That clearly demonstrates the NEED FOR REPENTANCE. Without repentance, a backslider will be condemned.

Galatians 2:17 - If, while we seek to be justified by Christ, we ourselves also are found sinners, is therefore Christ the minister of sin? God forbid. For if I build again the things which I destroyed, I make myself a transgressor.

TAKE HEED, BRETHERN...OF DEPARTING FROM THE LIVING GOD

Hebrews 3:12 - Take heed, brethren, lest there be in any of you an evil heart of unbelief, in departing from the living God.

Ezekiel 3:20 warns that if you turn from righteousness back to your sins, God may lay a STUMBLING BLOCK before you causing you to die in sin. Scripture warn of God's stumbling blocks.

Ezekiel 3:20 - When a righteous man doth turn from his righteousness, and commit iniquity, and I lay a stumbling block before him, he shall die: ...he shall die in his sin, and his righteousness which he hath done shall not be remembered.

Isaiah 54:17 – No weapon that is formed against thee shall prosper; and every tongue that shall rise against thee in judgment thou shalt condemn. This is the heritage of the servants of the LORD, and their righteousness is of me, saith the LORD.

Matthew 16:23 - But he turned, and said unto Peter, Get thee behind me, Satan: thou art an offence unto me: for thou savourest not the things that be of God, but those that be of men.

Jesus Christ is a CORNER STONE to those who believe. But Jesus is a STONE OF STUMBLING to those who disobey.

1 Peter 2:6-8 - Behold, I lay in Sion a chief corner stone, elect, precious: and he that believeth on him shall not be confounded. Unto you therefore which believe he is precious: but unto them which be disobedient, the stone which the builders disallowed, the same is made the head of the corner, And a stone of stumbling, and a rock of offence, even to them which stumble at the word, being disobedient: whereunto also they were appointed.

ARE YOU COACHABLE? DO YOU HAVE A TEACHABLE POSITION?

Like Father like Son – Apostolic Positioning

If you are a son (not just by gender, but through relationship), you should be manifesting in this season! If not, you are holding up everything around you.

What are you waiting on?

Roman 8:19 - *For the earnest expectation of the creature waiteth for the manifestation of the sons of God.*

Are you hearing from God? Or are you hearing from yourself?

John 12:49 - *For I have not spoken of myself; but the Father which sent me, he gave me a commandment, what I should say, and what I should speak.*

How do we answer to this? God is not sending us anywhere if we don't hear from him.

John 5:18 - *Then answered Jesus and said unto them, Verily, verily, I say unto you, The Son can do nothing of himself, but what he seeth the Father do: for what things soever he doeth, these also doeth the Son likewise.*

What is your spiritual Father speaking in this season? Are you in a good relationship? Who sent you?

_____

_____

_____

_____

_____

_____

_____

_____

_____

_____

_____

_____

_____

_____

Let us look at some Bible characters with the wrong spirit.

The spirit of Saul

1 Samuel 16:14 - But the Spirit of the LORD departed from Saul, and an evil spirit from the LORD troubled him.

How important it is to keep one's heart pure and sincere in the service of God, in spite of mistakes? When one falls from Heaven's favor, as a result of sin, he must pick himself up, and, in genuine contrition, return to the Creator's arms, tearfully seeking pardon. That was the difference between Saul and David (Psalm 32; 51). If we ignore our sins, they can, like a foreboding whirlpool, suck us into the depths of destruction. So it was with Israel's first king.

Watch out for the spirit a bad teammates.

Jude 1:10-11 - But these speak evil of those things which they know not: but what they know naturally, as brute beasts, in those things they corrupt themselves. Woe unto them! For they have gone in the way of Cain, and ran greedily after the error of Balaam for reward, and perished in the gainsaying of Core.

Characteristics of Rebellion:

- Seeking to overthrow the leader.
- Disputing the Leader's ability to effectively lead.
- Complaining against the Leader or his methods
- Causing Dissension or Division among the flock or you teammates.
- A spirit of defiance
- A back log of unconfessed offenses in the body.

- Spiritual blessings in activity of the Holy Spirit seems to be missing.
- Pride – in the form of activity seeking a place of leadership "Spotlight".
- Suggesting that the leader is not needed and unworthy to lead.
- Enticing others to follow rebellious suggestions.
- Counseling contrary to the word.
- Unwillingness to repent, individually or collectively.
- Refusing to be counseled when in error.

Confusion is caused by this orientation in the congregation and is the spirit of Core which bring distraction to the individuals, families, businesses, churches, and teams. Be careful how you let people affect you. Seek God for the gift of discernment. Don't allow anyone to position you against your Pastor, your spiritual coach. Be aware of complaining and don't allow someone with a bad spirit to persuade you. Mark those who cause division.

Romans 16:17 - Now I beseech you, brethren, mark them which cause divisions and offences contrary to the doctrine which ye have learned; and avoid them.

Take care that you will not be a "cut off" branch that is condemned to be cast into the fire.

NO MORE SACRIFICE FOR SIN

Hebrews 10:26-31 - For if we sin willfully after that we have received the knowledge of the truth, there remaineth no more sacrifice for sins, But a certain fearful looking for of judgment and fiery indignation, which shall devour the adversaries. He that despised Moses' law died without mercy under two or three witnesses: Of how much sorer punishment, suppose ye, shall he be thought worthy, who hath trodden underfoot the Son of God, and hath counted the blood of the covenant, wherewith he was sanctified, an unholy thing, and hath done despite unto the Spirit of grace? For we know him that hath said, Vengeance belongeth unto me, I will recompense, saith the Lord. And again, The Lord shall judge his people. It is a fearful thing to fall into the hands of the living God.

Chapter 3
The Finals of Life

The moment, day or time, you return into sin, "there remaineth no more sacrifice for sin." We must go back to God in repentance, and reappropriate the sacrifice of Jesus' blood. Until you repent, there is no blood sacrifice protecting you.

Hebrews 6:4-6 - For it is impossible for those who were once enlightened, and have tasted of the heavenly gift, and were made partakers of the Holy Ghost, And have tasted the good word of God, and the powers of the world to come, If they shall fall away, to renew them again unto repentance; seeing they crucify to themselves the Son of God afresh, and put him to an open shame.

RENEWED STRENGTH

As I understand this verse, nobody can possibly renew you to repentance if you have turned against God. The only possible hope I can imagine is if you, FROM THE DEPTHS OF YOUR OWN SOUL, come to your senses - as the Prodigal Son did - and as Jonah did in the belly of the whale - and RETURN TO YOUR FATHER with a broken and contrite spirit, and plead again for His mercy and grace.

We have to be godly sorry. We have to stop. Repentance mean return to the top. Come out of the low calling in answer to the high calling of Jesus Christ.

The preacher will not be able to reach you. The Spirit of God has stopped dealing with you. Until you decide that you are way off course with your life you have to return back to that through repentance.

(Note that this verse did not say it is impossible to be FORGIVEN. It said it is impossible to renew them again to repentance. You may be deaf to the preacher and the dealings of the Holy Spirit, but if you will wake yourself and turn to God, you may still be forgiven.)

The only possible way I can imagine you can be saved at this point is to have a personal, heart-felt awakening, and turn, and GO BACK TO GOD.

If you are such a state of mind, it is up to you. I am praying for anyone who is now in that sad and tragic condition - in Jesus' name.

HERE IS A PRAYER FOR BACKSLIDERS.

Lord, I pray for backsliders everywhere. Where there is life, there is hope. I pray for every Child of God who is "falling away," 2 Thessalonians 2:2, has become a castaway, 1 Corinthians 9:27, who has made shipwreck, 1 Timothy 1:19, who has forsaken, having loved this present world, 2 Timothy 4:10, for every prodigal, Luke 15:16, whose lamp has gone out, Matthew 25:8, whose salt has lost its savor, Matthew 5:13, whose candlestick may be removed, Revelation 2:5, and whose name may be blotted out of the Book of Life, Revelation 3:5. SAVE THEM, OH, LORD. Revive their souls today, in Jesus' name!

Lord, restore ALL our PRODIGAL children. Return ALL our backsliders to Righteousness and to your sheepfold. Wherever they are today, lead them back to Church and into fellowship with you and your people. Lord I pray, that you restore there soul lead them in the path of righteousness for your namesake.

Teach us how to walk in the spirit so we won't feel the last of the flash in Jesus name, Amen.

Once you have given your life to Christ, can you choose to turn away from the Lord? Can a converted person be lost?

_____

_____

_____

_____

_____

_____

_____

_____

_____

Christ speaks of those who "endure to the end" will be saved. This talk covers many Bible verses that discuss the ability we have to choose to turn away from God.

We can be disqualified. This book, "Finish Strong", highlights the Christian Race and how we have to stay in shape for the kingdom of God.

Believers have to follow the instructions and we have to stay our lane. We are living in the last days, the signs of the time are very evident. If Jesus Christ came back today, where will you spend eternity?

America is in trouble. We are experiencing moral decay and drug infestation. We are fighting an enemy that we cannot see. Billions of people go to church within the many religions worldwide. But there is ONE God, ONE faith, and ONE baptism.

The Bible tells us to study to show ourselves approved unto God a workman that need if not to be a shame to rightly dividing the word of truth.

Unlike many world religions...

Many religions focus on a person's spiritual efforts. With Jesus Christ it is a two-way interaction between us and God. He welcomes us to go to Him. "The Lord is near to all who call upon Him, to all who call upon Him in truth."

"You can communicate with God, who will answer your prayer, give you greater peace and joy, provide direction, show you his love, and transform your life. Jesus said, "I came that they might have life, and have it more abundantly." It will not mean that life will become perfect and free of problems. But it means that in the midst of life, you can relate to God who is willing to be involved in your life and faithful in his love.

"Finish Strong" is a book that will discipline your spirit man to stay in condition. It is compared to

an athlete versus our Christian race. There
are powerful scriptures that will take you to your goal
and help you press towards the mark of
the **prize** of the **high calling**, which is in Christ
Jesus. We must understand that we have to work out
our own soul salvation with fear and trembling, and
we can fall from grace out of the will of God into a
backslidden state.

We will discover some insightful scriptures that
we have to stay fit for the Kingdom of God, and stay
in relationship with God in His word that we can be
productive in our everyday life.

I pray that this book will be very insightful to
you, as it has been a blessing for me to finish. I want
to encourage by showing you how I disciplined myself
to maintain the strength to endure to the end. Stay
encouraged. You might be dealing with the
preliminaries of life or the semi-finals in life and you
are now ready for the finals of life. There are only
two destinations, heaven or hell.

I pray that this book prevents you from being
disqualified, or should I say, fallen out of the will of
God, or fallen from grace, or even in a back slidden
state. You will read the Truth, and it is the Truth that
will set you free.

I pray that this book is a blessing to you.

Luke 6:23 - When that happens, be happy! Yes, leap for joy! For a great reward awaits you in heaven! And remember, their ancestors treated the ancient prophets that same way.

Olympics 2016: Allyson Felix lost a gold medal to Shaunae Miller because of a dive. It's totally legal. American sprinter Allyson Felix would've had another Olympic gold medal instead of a silver if Shaunae Miller had stayed on her feet. Miller, a fantastic runner from the Bahamas, beat Felix in the women's Olympic 400-meter spring that Monday night by diving, belly-first, for the finish line. Miller came out of the blocks with a big lead on Felix. But as she approached the finish line, she seemed to run out of gas, with Felix breathing down her neck in the last few meters. So Miller dived, her torso crossing the finish line at 49.44 seconds, seven-hundredths of a second before Felix's 49.51.

Sometimes we are neck and neck with that satan. Many times he takes the lead. Whatever you do, whatever your trial, don't give up! Don't quit! We need to leap and finish strong!

God has a purpose for your pain, a reason for your struggles, and a reward for your faithfulness! Don't give up!!

Finish strong has to do with everyday living. We want to start off the day well and finish strong. Finish Strong has a lot to do with families. We want to be great parents, great fathers, and great mothers. We want to finish strong in our marriages.

These things are destined for us to accomplish in that we may finish strong in our endeavors. We want to continue to improve in our relationships with our friends and be an asset wherever we go, whatever we do for the Kingdom of God.

This book will encourage you on your endeavors to be an asset and to also make an impact. A lot of times we start off the race and we fall short of the glory or the goal. We fall short of victory. We're defeated when problems come.

The divorce rate is ridiculous. Trials and tribulations are on every hand. People are defeated because they lack the spiritual insight and also the far sight to accomplish the will of God. So, we need a coach, we need scripture, we need the truth in order to make it to the end, to make it to the goal. Finish Strong will encourage you as you have entered this Christian race to be the best that you can be; to be the best student, the best servant, the best Christian, the best leader, and to be the best person that you can be in this life on this side of life.

When it's all said and done, we will make it to heaven and receive the prize of eternity. This is so important to understand so we need to go into the scripture with an open heart and open spirit. Allow the Holy Spirit to minister to you throughout the scripture, these biblical truths are here to help you, to enlighten you, to be all that you can be in this Christian race.

I look back over my life when I was disqualified in so many different areas. As I stated in my book "From Sin & Shame to Glory", in Michigan I had problems. I brought my problems to Mississippi. My marriage had problems. I was almost disqualified as a husband. I was almost disqualified as a father. And I was almost disqualified as a servant of God.

So what does it profit a man to gain his whole world and lose his soul? We have to stay in condition. We have to work out our own soul salvation with fear and trembling. We have to continue to be dedicated to the things of God. We need strength training. We need to focus on our weaknesses. We need to improve over the hurdles of life when obstacles come. We need to increase our understanding, our wisdom, and our flexibility. We need to do what is required of us to stay in the race.

You don't stop when things don't go your way. You don't stop when disappointment appears. You don't stop when trials seem to be too heavy. You do not stop when you feel like it. You have to sacrifice, you have to get your body in shape, get your spirit in shape, and get motivated to the things of God.

This book will show you that you can run well and you can't be hindered. You can't be disqualified so God bless you. Read this book with an open mind and heart and I guarantee you that the spirit of the Lord will move in your life. It is my desire that every church and every pastor and every family will get a copy of this book to encourage them when times get low, when the race seems too long, when you get tired and fatigued and you get feel like giving up, and when you feel like you want to just sit down and sit back. This book will help you continue. It will help you if you're dealing with drug addiction. It will help you if you're dealing with problems in your marriage. This book will help you if you're dealing with problems as a new believer. It will help you get rooted into the ground in the truth. It is the truth of God that will set you free. And so, we want to encourage you, let these bible characters, let these scriptures and these parables be a great insight to your Christian race.

In closing out the year of 2016, I am very optimistic about 2017 being a new year. The number seven means perfection. Seven means completion. We must encourage ourselves with our endeavors to finish out the year strong.

It's very important that we set our eyesight on the prize of the high calling, looking unto Jesus who is the author and the finisher of our faith. It's going to take faith to have a better year. It's going to take faith to finish strong. We can capitalize on all our mistakes. We can learn from all our agonies and all our defeats. We can be all that we can be in this Kingdom race.

I want to encourage you as the time approaches to not stand still. This is an opportunity to seize the moment. Get your spirit man in condition. Eat right. Walk out with the spirit of perseverance and be determined to be what God called you to be.

In dealing with addictive behavior, it is easy to fall back into the trap and the snares of old living. You have to reconditioning yourself first in the Word of God. You have to be held accountable to a local church or held accountable by a spiritual leader, your spiritual guide, and most importantly, the Holy Spirit.

We want to stay committed to the cause, committed in the race. Once again, you might not be the very best, but you can do your best and God will do the rest. Let the weak say 'We're strong,' Amen! God wants to encourage you in the time of weaknesses. It is in the times of weakness when He can resort to our strengths. The strength for a Christian is to study the Word of God and to PRAY. The strength for a Christian is to be around other believers and to fellowship.

Be encouraged. Be determined. Praise God. Walk with the team, run with the team, and participate with the team.

MISTAKES CAN CAUSE YOU THE RACE

Rio Olympics

USA Track and Field's appeal of the disqualification of the men's 400-meter relay team has been denied, according to several reports.

The U.S. quartet finished third in the final on Friday August 19 2016, but soon afterward was disqualified because of a faulty baton exchange between leadoff runner Mike Rodgers and Justin Gatlin in which Rodgers passed it too early. Jamaica won, followed by Japan. Canada, which had finished fourth, was elevated to third following the U.S. disqualification. U.S. officials filed a protest with the Jury of Appeals of the International Assn. of Athletics Federations. The rejection of the appeal was first reported by Tim Layden of Sports Illustrated, who cited an official of the IAAF as saying all protests and appeals were rejected, leaving all results to stand. Associated Press also reported the protest had been rejected.

Luke 16:19-31 - There was a certain rich man, which was clothed in purple and fine linen, and fared sumptuously every day:

20 And there was a certain beggar named Lazarus, which was laid at his gate, full of sores,

21 And desiring to be fed with the crumbs which fell from the rich man's table: moreover the dogs came and licked his sores.

22 And it came to pass, that the beggar died, and was carried by the angels into Abraham's bosom: the rich man also died, and was buried;

23 And in hell he lift up his eyes, being in torments, and seeth Abraham afar off, and Lazarus in his bosom.

24 And he cried and said, Father Abraham, have mercy on me, and send Lazarus, that he may dip the tip of his finger in water, and cool my tongue; for I am tormented in this flame.

25 But Abraham said, Son, remember that thou in thy lifetime receivedst thy good things, and likewise Lazarus evil things: but now he is comforted, and thou art tormented.

26 And beside all this, between us and you there is a great gulf fixed: so that they which would pass from hence to you cannot; neither can they pass to us, that would come from thence.

²⁷ Then he said, I pray thee therefore, father, that thou wouldest send him to my father's house:
²⁸ For I have five brethren; that he may testify unto them, lest they also come into this place of torment.
²⁹ Abraham saith unto him, They have Moses and the prophets; let them hear them.
³⁰ And he said, Nay, father Abraham: but if one went unto them from the dead, they will repent.
³¹ And he said unto him, If they hear not Moses and the prophets, neither will they be persuaded, though one rose from the dead.

This story illustrates that once we cross the eternal horizon, that's it. There are no more chances. The transition to our eternal state takes place the moment we die (**2 Corinthians 5:8**; **Luke 23:43**; **Philippians 1:23**).

When believers die, they are immediately in the conscious fellowship and joys of heaven. When unbelievers die, they are just as immediately in the conscious pain, suffering, and torment of hell. Notice the rich man didn't ask for his brothers to pray for his release from some purgatorial middle ground, thereby expediting his journey to heaven. He knew he was in hell, and he knew why. That's why his requests were merely to be comforted and to have a warning sent to his brothers.

He knew there was no escape. He was eternally separated from God, and Abraham made it clear to him that there was no hope of ever mitigating his pain, suffering, or sorrow. Those in hell will perfectly recollect missed opportunities and their rejection of the gospel.

Jesus ultimately tells us the meaning behind the parable of the rich man and Lazarus. He was telling the Pharisees (who were self-righteous hypocrites) that since they did not truly believe and follow what Moses and the prophets wrote, no amount of miracles and wonders would be able to change their minds and alter how they lived life. It was the hardness of their hearts that kept them from truly repenting and serving God.

DRIVING IN THE FAST LANE – THE 8 MILE IN DETROIT

Walking from one side of Eight Mile Road to another is a jarring experience. To the south stretches Detroit, overwhelmingly black and poor. Businesses are shuttered. Some houses are burnt-out shells and abandoned cars stand on the streets.

To the north lies the mostly white suburbs of Oakland County. The shops are richer, the houses freshly painted, and the neighborhoods have names such as Ferndale and Royal Oak. In between stretches Eight Mile Road, so called because of its distance from Detroit's river front. It is a strip of highway lined by pawn brokers, sex shops, topless bars, fast food restaurants, and the sort of motels where guests stay either for an hour or three months.

It is a haven for prostitutes and drug dealers. Even at 9am, just pulling up to the side of the road is enough to elicit the attention of a young man keen to selling drugs. This is no environment that you or I want your children exposed to. I can only imagine how bad it is now. You didn't hear about HIV and other types of diseases in the 70s and 80s but what a tragedy when a young man or woman just curious gets involved in an environment such as the one where I escaped death.

I believe we are protected by the prayers of our loved ones, but why play Russian roulette with your life like I did? I did not die that day but I was already dead spiritually. We don't think about these things when we indulge in sinful activity.

Character should be measured by the Word of God, not by your familiar associations. People around you cannot influence you if they are just like you.

The area around Eight Mile has a lot to do with the people. Sin is everywhere. Every city is a modern day Sodom and Gomorrah. Crime rate has intensified.

The real significance of Eight Mile echoes far beyond Detroit. This eight-lane road is a dividing line. It is where the city of Detroit ends and the suburbs begin. It carves the rich from the poor, the black from the white, and the "have's" from the "have-not's". It symbolizes the death of urban America and the white flight to the suburbs. It signifies the plight of the impoverished, left behind in dying cities that cannot look after them. It is both a physical barrier and a psychological one.

Crossing Eight Mile Road is not as easy as just dodging the traffic. I can recall another near death experience driving on Woodword Ave in Detroit. I was high and intoxicated. It was late at night and my bad vision had my head blurred as I came to an intersection on Eight Mile Road. Here is what happened. As I came upon that intersection, in my drunken stupor, I pointed my finger out the window and pretended it was a gun. The person in the other car didn't find it humorous, and pointed a shotgun out their window. That could have ended it all. Needless to say, it sobered me up...quick.

These near death experiences are something that I completely ignored at the time. It could have been tragic, and I was unaware of what "grace" was. I was still living a half-hazard life. As a result, I began driving in the fast lane. I was having unprotected sex, bar hopping, free basing, and living a lifestyle of destruction.

I believe you can be at the wrong place at the wrong time and I also feel strongly that we can run out of grace. For you young people just getting started, evaluate yourselves and see that there is a better way. You do not have to put your dreams on hold. You can easily put your hand in the fire to know that it is hot. Take it from my experience, from my addiction, from my lifestyle of dysfunction; get saved and avoid the mistakes that I made. Be the man God calls you to be, be the woman God calls you to be.

I wrote this book, "Finish Strong", so you can save yourself from disqualification. This is a book of wisdom which is written to show you that we can't live our lives in the fast lane any longer. The young fall into graves as well as the old. But I thank God for the insight and strength given to us before death actually takes place.

The Bible says, "for the wages of sin is death, but the gift of God is eternal life". Choose life today. Choose life today. Choose to read this book in order to study and show yourself approved. Begin to work out your own soul salvation with fear and trembling. There is a lot of destruction, there is much around that corner that you do not want to experience.

The after hour bars, the drugs, the sexually transmitted diseases, the things you cannot recover from that will disqualify you are all waiting with open arms. But you do not have to walk in. There are a lot of people in the grave wishing they could have avoided that 8 mile and taken someone's advice. Take MY advice. You don't have to travel the same road I traveled. You do not have to go the distance that I went. God can save you if you want to be saved.

I just want to encourage you. I pray that you take a lap through the pages of life and discover Jesus Christ as your Lord and Savior.

CHRISTIAN RUNNERS

We arrange our life around certain disciplines that help us gain power and strength to become more like Jesus each day, to live a life as Jesus taught and modeled. The activities of prayer, Bible Study, worship, service, evangelism, and stewardship are among the needed disciplines for running the spiritual race.

- Prayer: How often are you talking with the Father each day?

- Bible Study: Are you engaged in a regular time of Bible reading, devotion, and study?

- Worship: Are you praising the Father in regular times of worship?

- Service: How are you using your gifts to serve God and his people?

- Evangelism: Have you spoken to someone recently regarding his or her relationship with God?

-     Stewardship: Are you investing regularly and consistently in God's church with your time, talents, and financial resources?

PREACHING NOTES

JESUS FINISHED STRONG

<u>Consider His Race</u> - His was a hard race that began in poverty and ended in pain on a cross. His was a race that lead Him around a track lined with hatred, bitterness, opposition and the desire to see Him dead. His was a race that set the perfect example of how a race should be run. His was a race in which He never faltered. He never lost sight of the goal and He never quit running until the goal had been achieved. When you feel like quitting, just look to Jesus and consider the race He ran for you and me. Then, run, Christian run!

<u>Consider His Reasons</u> - The Bible tells us here that Jesus ran "**FOR THE JOY THAT WAS SET BEFORE HIM**". Where is the joy in going to a cross? Where is the joy in dying like a common criminal? Where is the joy in being rejected by people you love? For Jesus, the joy was in what would happen when He finished His race. For Him, the joy was the day of redemption that would bring about the following:

1. The salvation of all believers
2. The day when He would be in Heaven with the redeemed of the ages.
3. The day when He would reclaim the glory He had shared with the Father from eternity past.

4. The day when there would be a new heavens and a new earth where all the redeemed would be worshiping the Father.

5. The day when salvation would be ultimately completed, sin forever destroyed, satan forever banished and perfect righteousness would rule in every heart.

That's why Jesus ran! He was able to look past the cross. He was able to despise the shame. He was able to think beyond everything He would be called upon to face in this world and He was able to see you. He ran His race for us. We are what motivated the heart of the Savior to go to that cross and die. We need to come to the place where we are able to look beyond the situations and circumstances of life and envision that day when we too will be home with the Savior. Oh, what a day that will be!! Glory to God, who will give you a second wind to be able to run your race with patience!

<u>Consider His Reward</u> - Jesus ran well and when He finished, He sat down with the Father on His throne! You see, Jesus knew where He was headed! That made it a little easier to run the race.

The same is true for you and me tonight. When we are able to get a heavenly vision, it makes the race more bearable. Hey, it's all a matter of perspective anyway!

Consider His Resolve - Jesus endured must to finish His race. Hey folks, He suffered more than you or I can grasp. A short list of things includes:

1. He was born to an unwed mother - Mt. 1:18-19
2. He was born in a stable - Lk. 2:7
3. Born to poor parents - Luke 2:24
4. His life was threatened as a baby - Matt. 2:13f
5. His birth was the cause of terrible suffering - Mt. 2:16ff
6. He was moved as a baby - Matt. 2:13ff
7. He was raised in a despicable town - Nazareth - Luke 2:39
8. His father died when He was young - Mt. 13:53-58
9. He had to support His family - Mt. 13:55-58
10. He had no home and no place to lay His head - Mt. 8:20; Luke 9:58
11. He was hated and opposed by others - Mark 14:1-2
12. He was charged with insanity - Mark 3:21
13. He was charged with demon possession - Mark 3:22
14. He opposed by His family - Mark 3:21-22
15. He was rejected, hated and opposed by the audiences who came to hear Him speak - Matt. 13:53-58; Luke 4:28-29.
16. He was betrayed by a close friend - Mark 14:10-11; 18
17. He was left alone, rejected and forsaken by all of His friends - Mark 14:50.
18. He was tried before the high court of the land and tried with treason - John 18:33.
19. He was executed as a common criminal by means of crucifixion - John 19:16

Have any of you ever suffered to that degree? Probably not! That is why we are told to compare our sufferings with His when we feel like giving up. He endured until the end so that we might be saved. He stands as our example. Therefore, let us run with patience the race that is set before us! You see, Jesus has already been around the track. That is why He is able to help us as we run.

Hebrews 4:15 - For we have not an high priest which cannot be touched with the feeling of our infirmities; but was in all points tempted like as we are, yet without sin.

RUNNING IN THE WRONG DIRECTION

Hell is a real place.

Isaiah 5:14 - Therefore hell hath enlarged herself, and opened her mouth without measure: and their glory, and their multitude, and their pomp, and he that rejoiceth, shall descend into it.

Christ finished the race.

Jesus Christ is number one, He has won the victory for us! All you have to do in the race to eternal life is to know, *if you finish, you win!*

The aging Apostle Paul said, "I have finished the race, I have kept the faith." What is the trophy? He says a "crown of righteousness" is awaiting me, and not for me only but for "all them that love his appearing."

Final lap: you must trust in His victory to be a winner in the race to eternal life.

Jesus is first..."the first born of many brethren." (Romans 8:29)

Salvation is to:
All who believe (Acts 13:39)
All who trust (2 Cor. 1:9)
All who continue (Jn. 8:31, Jn. 15:9, Acts 13:43, Rom. 11:22, Col. 1:23)
All who cleanse themselves (2 Cor. 7:1, 1 Jn. 1:9)
All who look for and love His appearing (1 Tim. 6:14, 2 Tim. 4:8, Titus 2:13)
All who call on His name (Acts 2:21. Rom. 10:13, 2 Tim. 2:22)

Rules in the race to eternal life:

God's Word says in 1 Corinthians 9:24, that if you are going to win the race it must be won **legally**; not by your opinion of God's rules, but what His Word says about Jesus. God's Word says that **Jesus is Lord**, and that you are a **sinner. Jesus** is **the only way to eternal life**. You are righteous only by His works, not your works.

Run to win! Strive to be the best. Forsake everything else to achieve your goal. Run legally. (1 Corinthians 9:24,25)

Faith in Jesus' work, continuing in pursuit of Christlikeness, and not fainting, causes you to Finish the Race, and if you finish, You Win!

Dear father God,

We humbly submit ourselves to you as our spiritual Guide in this Christian race. Thank you for your son Jesus Christ. As we enter this Christian Race, we vow to be honest with ourselves about our journey to the Kingdom of our Heavenly Father. Salvation can only be attained if we endure to the end.

Your word states:
James 1:12 - Blessed is the man that endureth temptation: for when he is tried, he shall receive the crown of life, which the Lord hath promised to them that love him.

Some are scoring themselves higher marks on a daily basis concerning their performance. They are so sure of their salvation regardless of their lifestyle. The race to salvation ends when we receive the glorious crown promised by our Lord, Jesus.

Matthew 24:13 - But he that shall endure unto the end, the same shall be saved.

If the Bible is to taken seriously, then we are still in the middle of the race to eternity. The crown of victory is for those who endure the persecutions of the atheists and agnostics to the end. Salvation is an ongoing process and cannot be achieved with little or no effort.

Even the lukewarm people and backsliders are claiming to have already secured their salvation in Christ. This is the word of the Apostle Paul in the Book of Philippians.

Philippians 3:12-14 - Not as though I had already attained, either were already perfect: but I follow after, if that I may apprehend that for which also I am apprehended of Christ Jesus.
13 Brethren, I count not myself to have apprehended: but this one thing I do, forgetting those things which are behind, and reaching forth unto those things which are before,
14 I press toward the mark for the prize of the high calling of God in Christ Jesus.

It is better to remain focused and ignore all sorts of distractions so that we may press on toward the goal than to be self-assured of what is not yet attained.

A good start does not guarantee a great finish. Now, unto Him that is able to keep us from falling and to present us faultless before the presence of His glory with exceeding joy, to the only wise God, our Savior, be glory and majesty, dominion and power, both now and forever, AMEN.

If you prayed this prayer and if this book is a blessing to you please email me your thoughts.

pastorcflow@aol.com

Author Apostle Carl Flowers

I just beat a personal record in my walk!

Workout: Walk
Date: Sep 5, 2016
Distance: 15.65 mi
Duration: 5:16:10

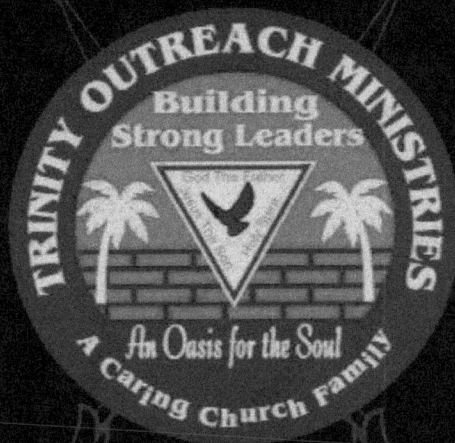

TRINITY OUTREACH MINISTRIES

Building
Strong Leaders

An Oasis for the Soul

A Caring Church Family

502 Jarrell St, Picayune, MS 39466
Apostle Carl Flowers & Julie Flowers

About the Author

Pastor Carl Flowers is the Founder and President of Trinity Outreach Ministries in Picayune, Mississippi. He is also the Founder of the Oasis Community Development Center in Picayune, Mississippi. Pastor Flowers is the instructor of the ARRM Restoration Recovery Ministry and Director of the Covenant Bible College and Seminary Satellite Campus, which is designed to educated and strengthen the body of Christ by identifying their purpose in helping those struggling with addiction.

Pastor Flowers is a speaker, spiritual father to many, and a mentor. He and his wife, Julie, and the two children born of their union reside in Picayune, Mississippi.

For speaking engagements on recovery, please contact **pastorcflow@aol.com**

www.ingramcontent.com/pod-product-compliance
Lightning Source LLC
Chambersburg PA
CBHW062000040426
42447CB00010B/1844